My War

Home Guard

Philip Steele

HODDER
Wayland

an imprint of Hodder Children's Books

Produced for Hodder Wayland by
Discovery Books Ltd
Unit 3, 37 Watling Street, Leintwardine, Shropshire SY7 0LW

First published in 2003 by Hodder Wayland, an imprint of Hodder Children's Books

British Library Cataloguing in Publication Data
Steele, Philip, 1948-
Home Guard. - (My war)
1. Great Britain. Army. Home Guard 2. World War, 1939-1945 -
War work - Great Britain - Juvenile literature 3. Great Britain -
History - George VI, 1936-1952 - Juvenile literature
I. Title
940.5'316'0941

ISBN 0 7502 4221 3

Printed and bound in Italy by Canale & C.S.p.A. Turin

Series editor: Gianna Williams
Designer: Ian Winton
Picture research: Rachel Tisdale

Hodder Children's Books would like to thank the following for the loan of their material:
Corbis: p.25; Discovery Picture Library: p.15; Hulton Archive: pp.10 (top), 12, 13, 16, 18, 19, 20, 28;
Hulton-Deutsch Collection/Corbis: pp.6, 10 (bottom), pp.14, 17, 21, p.22, 23; Imperial War Museum:
cover (men on motorbike), p. 7; Robert Opie Collection: p. 27
Cover: Imperial War Museum (men on motorbike), group photograph from personal collection
of Charles Dibbons.

Discovery Books would like to thank the following for their help:
Iorwerth Jones, Charles Dibbons, Gerry Knight, Noel Cliff, Eric Ross,
Jenny Scolding/Serpentine Design and Ann Dickie.

Hodder Children's Books
A division of Hodder Headline Limited
338 Euston Road
London NW1 3BH

Contents

Meet the Home Guard

In 1939 Britain went to war against Germany. The brutal Nazi Party which ruled Germany had ordered its troops into Central Europe, the Netherlands, Belgium and France. By May 1940 British troops in mainland Europe were being pushed back to the Channel ports. Many people feared that the Germans would soon try to invade Britain.

The British government decided to call upon all men not already serving in the armed forces to become part-time

NOEL CLIFF

Noel was 19 years old in 1940. Until 1942, when he joined the regular army, he spent many hours on the look-out for a German invasion force on the coast of Cornwall.

IORWERTH JONES

Iorwerth was born in 1911, on the Isle of Anglesey in North Wales. He had served in the army before the war, but had left because of a bad sports injury. Even so, his experience of soldiering was useful in the Home Guard.

soldiers. In this book, five of these 'Local Defence Volunteers', later known as the Home Guard, recall their memories of the Second World War.

GERRY KNIGHT

Gerry, born in 1920, was from Epsom in the south-east of England. In 1941 he joined up with a Home Guard unit at the college where he was studying, at Isleworth in Middlesex.

CHARLES DIBBONS

Charles was born on the Isle of Wight in 1917. He joined up with the top secret Auxiliary Unit – a division of the Home Guard which was designed to work as an underground army in the event of a German invasion.

ERIC ROSS

Dr Eric Ross was born in 1920 in Perthshire, Scotland. In 1940, while he was a medical student in Edinburgh, he joined the Local Defence Volunteers. Like the others he was ready to do his bit.

Early Days

On 14 May 1940 the War Minister, Anthony Eden, announced that local forces were to be set up across Britain. He called upon men to join their Local Defence Volunteers (LDV). Their job would be to guard important installations and to watch out for invading commandos or paratroopers.

Within hours volunteers were queuing up at local police stations and halls. About 250,000 men signed up on the next day alone. Some of those who joined were too young to serve in the regular army yet. Even more were too old, having fought in the First World War (1914-18) or even earlier conflicts.

◄ Londoners queue at a police station to sign on with the newly formed Local Defence Volunteers in May 1940.

NOEL

At the end of May 1940, British troops had to be evacuated from the French port of Dunkirk. It was just after that that I decided I had to join the LDV. The only defence we had against the Germans was broomsticks, pitchforks and old shotguns which were unfit to be fired. We had no uniform, just khaki armbands saying LDV.

IORWERTH

In 1934, when I was stationed in Gibraltar with the Royal Welch Fusiliers, a leg injury put paid to my soldiering. It kept me in hospital for two years. I was back in Wales when war broke out and didn't think I'd be much use. But my friend Idris Davies, from the village garage, persuaded me to join up. 'Your experience could be useful,' he said, 'and anyway, we'll have a laugh...'

Many of those who joined up were people who could not join the regular army because their daytime jobs were necessary to keep the country running. They included railway workers, bakers, grocers, bank staff and teachers.

▼ Although still wearing their everyday clothes, these recruits wear LDV armbands and stand smartly to attention on parade. Army veterans display their medals.

From LDV to Home Guard

The LDV met in halls and huts and offices. Seeing the old boys from earlier wars parading alongside teenagers, people made up unkind nicknames: 'Last Desperate Venture', 'Long-Dentured Veterans' or 'Look, Duck and Vanish'. Perhaps that was why the Prime Minister, Winston Churchill, decided to change their name to the Home Guard in July 1940.

NOEL

It was all talk about 'invasion' in those early days, but I don't think they had much idea about what kind of invasion it would be. We were meant to be defending the beach at Kennack Sands, but in reality the Germans could only have got a couple of tanks ashore at that point.

Soon proper uniforms began to arrive, although they were often a poor fit. The new recruits marched and drilled and soon began to shape up.

◀ Noel Cliff wears the serge 'battledress', used for parades. Denim uniforms were worn for work duties.

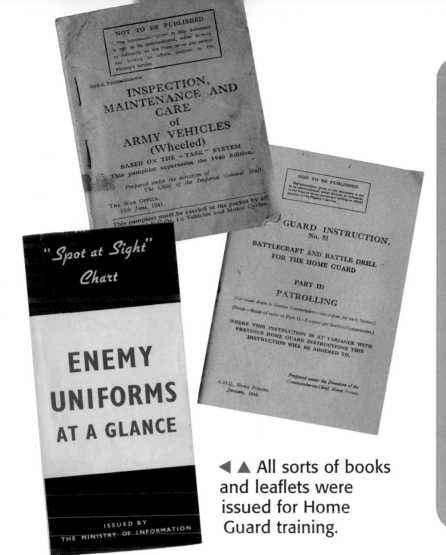

IORWERTH

Our Home Guard unit met in Llangoed village hall. Because of my experience in the army I could help out with the drill and weapons training. The lads actually enjoyed the drilling, you know. A couple of them never did quite get the hang of it, but most of them were first rate.

◀ ▲ All sorts of books and leaflets were issued for Home Guard training.

By August 1940 the skies of southern England were full of battling fighter planes, and in the autumn British cities came under massive German bombing attacks. Although people joked about the Home Guard, everyone understood that invasion was now a real danger.

ERIC

I had no military training at all when I joined. My father hadn't even agreed to my belonging to the Cadet Corps at school. Still, a lot of men had seen action in the 1914-18 war. They were still in their forties and were quite fit. On joining, I was issued with a Canadian Ross rifle and just three rounds of ammunition [three bullets].

Special or Secret Units

Some Home Guards formed special units of cyclists or horseback riders. Others used motor launches to patrol rivers. Some units recruited women to help with driving, catering, office work and communications.

▲ One of the first women's platoons in the Home Guard march down Whitehall, in London. They have yet to be issued with uniforms.

▲ A patrol defends a riverbank on Dartmoor, Devon, in 1941. They were trained in camouflage and guerrilla warfare.

Mounted Home Guard units were useful in patrolling uplands such as Dartmoor, the Yorkshire Moors or the mountains of South Wales.

In 1940 special Auxiliary Units were set up in areas of likely invasion. Auxiliary just means 'support' and the public was led to believe that these were just normal Home Guards. In reality they formed top-secret units, trained in sabotage, explosives and hand-to-hand combat. They built hidden bunkers in the countryside and learned to live off the land. These men were meant to be the backbone of the resistance after an invasion.

CHARLES

I was a keen Sea Scout as a boy. My friend 'Rap' was a Rover Scout leader and he sounded me out. The next thing I knew, an army officer dressed in 'civvies' came knocking at my door. Would I be interested in helping my country? Could I keep a secret?

We were given training lectures at Wotton Town Hall and then we had to go out and put into practice what we had learned. We were taught to use weapons and explosives and to survive off the land. I couldn't even tell my mother what I was getting up to. Some of my friends in the unit would never tell a soul about their wartime activities, even when the war had been over for years.

◀ Charles Dibbons (kneeling on left) and his auxiliary unit trained on the Isle of Wight as part of a secret army.

More Like an Army

At its greatest strength, the Home Guard numbered about 1.5 million men. As in the regular army, sections were grouped together within platoons, platoons within companies and companies within battalions. These were mostly based on villages or towns, districts and larger regions.

Some units were based on the workplace. For example, dockers and other workers for the Port of London Authority formed their own Home Guard units.

IORWERTH

Our unit was drawn from three small villages: Llangoed, Penmon and Glan-yr-afon. We were commanded by Major Arnold, who was a farmer and local magistrate. He had served in the 1914-18 war. He was well liked and would share a drink with us in the pub.

▶ These Home Guards belong to a special Post Office section. They could not join the regular army, because letters still needed delivering. Here they are learning how to handle a Lewis gun while on a summer camp in 1943.

GERRY

Our unit numbered at least 60. It was formed by the teacher training college at Isleworth in Middlesex and included teachers, students and college workers. Some of them had been in the regular army. I was given one stripe [the rank of lance corporal] because I had been an army cadet.

Ranks in the Home Guard matched those of the regular army. If people had already served as a soldier they might now be made lance corporal, corporal or sergeant.

▶ These fishermen from Holy Island, in the north-east of England, have also formed their own Home Guard unit.

CHARLES

It was different in the auxiliaries. We were only seven to a unit, each led by a sergeant. We did meet up with other units, but none of us was allowed an overall view of the organization. That way, we couldn't pass on information if we were captured. We wore uniforms – we had to if we were to be treated as proper soldiers under the Geneva Convention – but we didn't have parades.

Weapons and Defence

Gradually the farmers' shotguns and home-made weapons used by the LDV were replaced by working .303 rifles and supplies of ammunition. Home Guards learned how to fix bayonets and charge with what they hoped were blood-curdling yells to terrify the enemy. There were also a few precious anti-tank weapons and automatic weapons such as machine guns.

▲ Home Guards learned how to use mortars and grenades and also how to produce a wide variety of home-made weapons and bombs.

GERRY

I was made responsible for 'intelligence' and one of my duties was to explain the use of new weapons to the unit. One morning a new mortar arrived. I only had until 11 o'clock to work it out for myself before instructing the others! I was training to be a teacher, so I suppose it was good practice for that!

In some areas the Home Guards faced real danger. There was heavy bombing in many cities. Even in the countryside there were enemy aircraft which had come down and, by the summer of 1944, deadly flying bombs nicknamed 'doodlebugs'.

NOEL

We managed to get a selection of working rifles, some Belgian, some French. We had one Hotchkiss machine gun.

There were concrete blocks set up against tanks and alongside the roads we set up pipes of petrol with holes in them. These formed jets which could be set alight to stop invaders getting through.

◄ 'Pill boxes' are still dotted all over the British countryside. These small fortifications of brick and concrete were meant to be used as firing positions and stores in case of invasion.

► *Could You Please Oblige Us With A Bren Gun?* In July 1941 songwriter Noel Coward poked fun at the Home Guard's lack of modern weapons in the early days. He exaggerated a bit – an arquebus was a type of gun used in the 1500s and the Battle of Waterloo was fought in 1815!

'Could you please oblige us with a bren gun?
Or, failing that, a hand grenade will do.
We've got some ammunition
In a rather damp condition,
And Mayor Huss
Has an arquebus
That was used at Waterloo.'

Duties and Patrols

Home Guards were expected to give up two or three nights a week and most weekends to duties. These included patrols, road blocks to check identity papers, guarding ammunition dumps or important installations such as gasworks. Enemy aircraft which had been shot down needed to be located and the pilots captured. Basic German phrases were learned, but often none too accurately.

IORWERTH

With my injury I could not patrol on foot, but I could get around when there was transport. Sometimes we could see flashes from the bombing of Liverpool over the horizon.

▶ A German bomber is shot down in Sussex in 1940, during the Battle of Britain. The Home Guard capture the pilots, who have parachuted to safety.

Sometimes local people did not take the Home Guard seriously and ignored their commands – but at their peril.

▼ The Southern Railway Home Guard man an anti-aircraft gun, protecting the track and goods yards from enemy attack.

ERIC

On 15 September 1940 the church bell rang, which was the signal for us all to turn out. We were sent off to guard a bridge by a graveyard, miles from anywhere. In the middle of the night we heard footsteps. 'Halt! Who goes there?' we shouted. 'Och laddie, I've nae time for this nonsense,' came the reply in a broad Scottish accent. We reckoned no German could have perfected the language to this degree, so we said: 'Pass, friend!'

NOEL

There was a machine gun emplacement up at Gwendreath with a couple of soldiers from the Manchester regiment. One Home Guard chap had to go up there each night – they needed local knowledge of short cuts and back paths in case they had to get out quick. I went up there and squeezed through the hedge. They pounced on me and put a bayonet to my throat. It was very real, you know. That was the night the Germans bombed Falmouth and hit the oil tanks. The whole of Cornwall was lit up.

Mock Battles

Much of the Home Guards' time was spent on operations such as cross-country manoeuvres at night time, which were meant to train them for real action. Mock battles were held in which local units would 'fight' each other, aiming to capture or 'kill' the enemy, perhaps by marking them with a red dye.

▶ Home Guards practise combat techniques with fixed bayonets – in a far from realistic situation. They would have laughed if they weren't too busy yelling.

GERRY

Our greatest battle was an 'attack' on the Mogden sewage works! Our unit was ordered to capture the reservoirs and a neighbouring unit had to defend the walls. My job was to go back and forth gathering intelligence about the enemy's positions.

Bags of flour would be hurled instead of grenades. Blank ammunition would be fired. An officer would observe the action and then declare which unit had won.

These battles were serious training exercises, but of course they gave rise to many humorous incidents. Men from one village played tricks on another, or the officer would be attacked and captured by mistake.

▼ An 'enemy' spy tries in vain to get through a road block, during a combined police and Home Guard exercise in 1941.

IORWERTH

The lads from our village had to invade the neighbouring town of Beaumaris. A story went around the village that they hijacked the local bus and hid under the seats. The bus was waved through the road block outside the town, and so they got through the enemy lines and had a famous victory, without a 'shot' being fired.

Sticky Moments

Humorous stories about the exploits of the Home Guard soon passed around every village and town in the country.

People laughed about the local grocer running out into the street in his pyjamas when a German plane came low overhead, or the air-raid warden in his tin hat, blowing a whistle, pedalling up and down furiously on his bicycle.

CHARLES

As auxiliaries we had to learn how to survive off the land. We were shown how to catch rabbits for food and told to steal crops growing in the fields. One evening I was walking along the road with a sack of illegal vegetables when the local policeman stopped for a chat. There was I trying to hide the sack behind my back and talk innocently. It seemed to take an age until he carried on walking his beat.

◄ Home Guards had to practise whatever the weather. This time they are in a snowy British field in winter.

Blunders were common and some could have been serious. One Cornish Home Guard unit was practising firing out to sea. They did not realize that the Royal Navy had a ship out of sight, below the cliff edge. Soon the ship was returning fire at the cliff top with all its guns ablaze.

▶ Is it a tree? No, it's a Home Guard, practising camouflage techniques on a North London golf course in 1941. Exercises like this caused great amusement at the time.

NOEL

My friend Bernard Dale was a runner for the Home Guard, carrying messages between the units. He went over to St Keverne where they were all sitting in the hut having a drink. They asked him to fill the paraffin lamps and trim the wicks. He topped them up, but there was some paraffin left in the can. 'Put it in the barrel in the cupboard,' he was told. He did so, but it turned out there were two barrels – one for paraffin and one for beer. You can guess what happened next!

Life in Wartime

The war years were a time of hardship for all. Rationing was brought in to limit the amount of goods such as food, clothing and petrol that the public could buy. People now wore simple clothes even when they got married, although some brides made traditional white dresses from spare ends of parachute cloth.

GERRY

There was some danger, I suppose, but you just got used to it. There was anti-aircraft fire and bombing, but you still went out to get fish-and-chips for other members of the unit and thought nothing of it. There wasn't much time left for entertainments.

IORWERTH

After air raids on Liverpool, German planes sometimes dropped off unused bombs along the coast of North Wales before flying home. One offshore explosion off Anglesey blew up a huge shoal of herrings. We collected them off the beach. They were perfectly good to eat.

▲ At a training camp in 1941, members of the Home Guard line up for a morning shave before going on parade.

Home Guards still had to do their normal jobs, and this left little time for leisure. The younger ones enjoyed going to dances at local halls and meeting up with 'land girls' who had moved to the area, or with young women in the forces.

However the older Home Guards and those with families looked for little more entertainment than a glass of beer at the local pub.

◄ A Home Guard patrol stops by a farm for a warming cup of tea, during the Christmas holiday of 1940.

Moving On

The chief aim of the Home Guard was the defence of Britain against invasion. However it also came to serve another purpose, in training young men for the regular army. As the war continued, many of the teenage volunteers of 1940 were called up for full-time service in army regiments.

GERRY

I left the Home Guard, but my experience was useful as I became involved with another branch of military training, working as an instructor of army cadets.

ERIC

Having studied to be a doctor, I became part of the Royal Medical Corps when I joined up.

▶ Dr Eric Ross poses with nurses. In joining the army, he combined his medical studies with his Home Guard experience.

▶ On D-Day, 6 June 1944, British, American and Canadian troops landed on the coast of Normandy, in German-occupied France. Noel Cliff went ashore three days later, but the beach where he landed was still being shelled by the enemy.

Their enemy was no longer the Home Guard unit from the next village, but battle-hardened troops in foreign lands. However anxious they may have been on leaving home, most of them soon found that the time they had spent in the LDV and the Home Guard proved to be very useful. They were already trained to drill, to use weapons and to think like soldiers.

NOEL

I left the Home Guard in 1942, when I was called up into the regular army, where I repaired vehicles. I landed with the troops in Normandy and went on through France, Belgium and Holland. I was outside the German town of Lüneberg when the peace treaty was eventually signed on Lüneberg Heath, in 1945.

CHARLES

I was called up near the end of the war. I was based in Gibraltar, providing water transport for Combined Operations in the North Africa campaign.

The Road to Peace

The D-Day landings marked the last phase of the war in Europe. The Allies began to push the German army eastwards.

NOEL

After the war I came back to Cornwall and worked at the Culdrose air base, then for Vickers Armstrong engineering at Predannack. I still live in my home village of Ruan Minor. I enjoy painting and I organize a vintage car and steam traction engine rally each year.

CHARLES

I came back to the Isle of Wight after the war and took up my old job of shipwright. I got married in 1950.

IORWERTH

During the war I worked for the Sanders Roe factory at Llanfaes. They made and repaired Catalina flying boats. My job was replacing the guns on them. After the war, the company turned to making buses and coaches and I worked on the fittings and trimmings.

Flying bombs were pounding south-east England, but by that autumn it was becoming clear that the war was nearly won. No longer needed, the Home Guard was officially 'stood down', or disbanded, in November 1944.

Daily Mail

VICTORY EDITION

TUESday FIELD-DAY

NO. 15,290   ONE PENNY   ★ ★ ★   FOR KING AND EMPIRE   TUESDAY, MAY 8, 1945

3 POWERS WILL ANNOUNCE GREAT SURRENDER SIMULTANEOUSLY

VE-DAY—IT'S ALL OVER

The King to speak to Empire: Victorious generals will follow Premier on radio

Joy-day throngs stop traffic

IN NEW YORK

All Britain stood by for news

How it broke—hour by hour

▲ On 8 May 1945, newspapers joyfully reported that Germany had surrendered to the Allied forces. Victory in Europe was marked by wild celebrations.

On 8 May 1945, a date remembered as VE (Victory in Europe) Day, the German army surrendered. The Second World War finally ended on 15 August 1945 (VJ or Victory over Japan Day). Home Guards who had gone into the regular army now returned home and met up with comrades from their old units. Life slowly returned to normal.

GERRY

After the war I decided not to become a teacher after all. In 1946 I joined British European Airways and I worked in airport management until I retired. I now live in the village of Brockham, in Surrey.

Looking Back

Over the years the humorous tales told about the Home Guard were often better remembered than the serious work they carried out.

Dad's Army wasn't far off the mark. But I have no doubt if an invasion had taken place, they would have put up a good fight. They were well trained and became a serious fighting force.

In the 1970s they became the subject of a very popular television comedy called *Dad's Army* which is still often shown today.

▲ The cast of *Dad's Army* managed to capture the mood of the 1940s. Their catchphrases, such as 'Don't panic, Mr Mainwaring!' are still repeated today.

GERRY

The Home Guard would have resisted well, but I don't think they would have been able to hold back an invasion for more than a couple of days. The regular army itself would have been very stretched.

However, the training of the Home Guards and the Auxiliary Units really was quite effective. They would not have been able to stop an invasion, nor were they expected to. But after the early days, they could have been very valuable in delaying enemy troops and in forming a resistance. King George VI admitted that the Home Guards were poorly equipped for war 'against the most powerful army in the world' but praised them for being 'mighty in courage and determination'.

NOEL

We had great comradeship, you know. Wars are foolish, but I do think this was a just war, which most of the wars fought today are not. If ever there was evil, it was under the rule of the Nazis.

▶ King George VI's Final Message to the Home Guard was broadcast on 3 December 1944, after they had marched past him in London for their last parade.

'I believe it is the voluntary spirit which has always made the Home Guard so splendid and so powerful a comradeship of arms.'

ERIC

I am glad that I served. Today's children should learn about wars and be glad that Hitler was defeated. Looking back, I do remember thinking that war was horrible and futile, that we should not do such terrible things to each other as human beings. I just hope that children living today never have to experience war for themselves.

Glossary

Air-raid warden an official responsible for public safety during wartime bombing.

Allies the troops of those countries fighting Germany, Italy and Japan during the Second World War.

Battalion a military unit made up of three or more companies.

Battledress the army uniform normally worn for drilling and battle.

Bayonet a long blade which can be attached to the end of a rifle for hand-to-hand fighting.

Bren gun a type of light machine gun used in the Second World War.

Bunker a fortified underground shelter or control centre, used in wartime.

Camouflage ways of concealing people, buildings or weapons from attackers, by making their colours blend in with their background.

'Civvies' normal ('civilian') clothes rather than an army uniform.

Commando a member of a unit of specially trained troops.

Company a military unit made up of several platoons, part of a battalion.

'Doodlebugs' a nickname for flying bombs, unmanned rockets launched against targets in Britian during the Second World War.

Evacuate to transport people away from danger.

Gasworks a factory which produces and stores gas for use in industry or homes.

Gelignite an explosive used to blow up rocks or buildings.

Geneva Convention one of the international agreements deciding how prisoners of war should be treated.

Installation place or building.

Intelligence military information.

Khaki a brown-green colour.

Land girl a nickname for any member of the Women's Land Army, women volunteers who worked the land left by farmers who had gone to fight in the war.

Manoeuvre a movement of troops during a battle or a training exercise.

Mortar a short-barrelled cannon which can fire shells at a high angle.

Nazi short for 'National Socialist', a German political party which became powerful in the 1930s. The Nazis were ruthless and violent, and would not allow any opposition.

Paratrooper a member of the parachute regiment.

Pillbox a small fortification of brick or concrete, used to provide cover for firing weapons.

Plastic explosive a putty-like explosive, such as cyclonite, which can be used to make home-made bombs.

Platoon a military unit made up of two or more sections, part of a company.

Racist believing that one part of the human race is superior to another part. The Nazis who ruled Germany believed that Jews, Roma (Gypsies) and Slavs were inferior people.

Rationing laws brought in because of wartime shortages which limited the amount of goods one person could buy. Food, clothing, petrol and many other items were rationed.

Regular army the main British army, as opposed to the part-time Home Guard.

Resistance a group of people, not belonging to an official army, who fight troops occupying their country.

Sabotage damage to machines or vehicles caused by enemy agents or resistance fighters during wartime.

Serge a thick, rough woollen cloth.

Stand down to release troops from duty, to disband a unit.

Tin hat a simple metal helmet.

Tommy gun a nickname for a submachine gun (from a make of gun called Thompson).

Volunteer someone who offers to do something of their own free will.

Further Reading

Non-fiction

Fyfield, Frances, *The Home Front*, Heinemann Library, 1995.

Robson, Pam and York, John, *All About the Second World War 1939-45,* Hodder Wayland, 1996.

Ross, Stewart, History Through Newspapers: *The Home Front in World War II,* Hodder Wayland, 2002.

Smith, Nigel, *Family Life: Second World War,* Hodder Wayland, 1998.

Fiction

Hayer, Rosemary, *The Fox in the Wood: a Wartime Adventure*, Anglia Young Books, 1995.

Swindell, Robert, *Hurricane Summer*, Mammoth, 1997.

Swindell, Robert, *Roger's War*, Mammoth, 1999.

Resources

Books

Carroll, David, *Dad's Army: the Home Guard 1940-1944,* Sutton, 2002

SP Mackenzie. *The Home Guard,* Oxford University Press, 1995

Audio Cassettes

Shaw, Frank et al, *We Remember the Home Guard,* Isis Audio Books, 1998

Places to Visit

The Imperial War Museums in London (Lambeth) and the North (Manchester) are the best places to find out about life in Britain during the Second World War.

Index

Numbers in *italics* indicate photographs.